This book belongs to the kind and amazing...

Printed in Great Britain
by Amazon

55222881R00174